Workbook Answer Key

1 Impressions

Grammar

1

a 1 c 4 e 3 g 7
b 6 d 8 f 2 h 5

2

1 just bought
2 was walking
3 saw
4 had been looking
5 was selling
6 used to have
7 always feel
8 'm wearing

3

a So does Venice.
b So is *Titanic*.
c Neither has Jodie Foster.
d So did Daniel Day-Lewis.
e So does Kiefer Sutherland.
f Neither has Antonio Banderas.
g Neither was Schwarzenegger.
h So did Tom Hanks.

Sentences **c**, **f**, and **h** are completely untrue.

4

a So do I. / I don't!
b So have I. / I haven't!
c So would I. / I wouldn't!
d Neither do I. / I do!
e Neither do I. / I do!
f So am I. / I'm not!
g So did I. / Ididn't!
h Neither have I. / I have!
i Neither could I. / Icould!

5

a weren't you R
b aren't you F
c are you F
d do you R
e don't you R
f didn't you F
g can you R
h have you F
i did you F

6

a doesn't she
b did I
c aren't I
d haven't you
e was it
f does she
g do they

7

a Do you know what kind of salary you are looking for?
b Could you tell me which political party you vote for?
c Do you think that you work well under stress?
d Do you mind telling me if/ whether you have ever been in trouble with the police?
e I'd like to know what is more important for you: money or job satisfaction.
f Would you say that you are a "morning person" or an "afternoon person"?
g I'd like to know whether you believe in God.

Pronunciation

a Speaker A
b Speaker A
c Speaker B
d Speaker B
e Speaker A
f Speaker B

Vocabulary

1

Usually positive characteristics: warm, charming, hearty, sparkling

Usually negative characteristics: abrasive, fake, harsh, shrill, strident

2

a 6 c 2 e 1 g 3
b 5 d 4 f 7

3

a charming
b firm
c impassive
d forced
e staring
f spiky
g husky
h designer

4

a rearrange
b reconstruct
c rethink
d reword
e remake
f redo
g repackage
h re-examine

5

a cuff
b button
c belt
d sleeve
e buckle

6

1 c 3 a 5 b
2 d 4 e

7

1 guess
2 can't
3 down
4 up
5 annoying

8

1 that
2 over
3 one
4 with
5 image
6 bears
7 resemblance
8 same
9 recognize
10 looks
11 like
12 looki

Writing

1

c A voice and a life

2

1 b 2 c 3 a

3

I first discovered her music because my mother used to like it and listen to it when she was cooking. About ten years ago, Marianne Faithfull was in concert here, and we went together. She was superb. I love the way she sings, and she has had such a fascinating life. I don't like everything that she has done, but she's always interesting.

4

appeared beautiful concert
different extremely
fascinating favorite including
interesting recently serious

2 Generations

Grammar

1

a making
b Let
c force
d allow
e get
f arrange
g attempt
h mind
i ask

2

a to understand
b talking
c going
d to help
e spending
f to leave
g know
h to give

3

a They couldn't afford to buy lots of new clothes.
b They encouraged me to go to church every week.
c They never let me bring friends home.
d They made me come home at ten o'clock every night.
e They warned me not to go to nightclubs because they were dangerous.
f My father expected me to work in his factory.
g My parents taught me to respect authority.
h I was dreading telling my parents that I had a boyfriend.
i I managed to run away from home when I was 15.
j I tried to live on my own, but it was very hard.

4

1 at
2 to
3 in
4 at
5 for
6 about
7 to
8 of
9 with
10 with

5

a Do you find it difficult to get up in the morning?
b Is it embarrassing for you to speak English?
c Do you find it irritating to get spam email?
d Is it easy for you to keep a secret?
e Do you find it boring to watch commercials on TV?
f Do you find it amusing to look at old family pictures?

Vocabulary

1

a dreading
b aiming
c avoid
d manage
e urged
f warned
g mind
h encourage

2

a Charity begins at home.
b Blood is thicker than water.
c Home is where the heart is.
d Birds of a feather flock together.
e Two's company, three's a crowd.
f One good turn deserves another.

3

1 a
2 f
3 e
4 d
5 c
6 b

4

a impressed
b fed up
c irritating
d terrible
e optimistic
f allergic
g amazed

5

a terrible
b allergic
c amazed
d impressed
e optimistic
f irritating
g fed up

6

1 take
2 call
3 have
4 welcome
5 make
6 show
7 help
8 holler

Pronunciation

1

a gray, say, chase, fake
b buy, try, flight, wild
c boy, toy, annoy, join
d go, know, clothes, host
e how, now, clown, ground

2

a lost
b wear
c give
d low
e have

Listening

1

Speaker 1: Picture c

Speaker 2: Picture b

Speaker 3: Picture a

2

	Speaker		
topic	1	2	3
entertainment	✓	✓	
marriage			✓
politics		✓	
money		✓	✓
studies	✓		✓
work	✓		✓

3

a a bad job
b not as good as people claim
c caused things to go wrong
d made very easy for them
e survive financially
f a situation where you have two very different advantages

3 Gold

Grammar

1

a he had just won
b he had won; he was going to do
c he didn't know; he would buy
d would use up
e he wanted
f she wanted
g they were going
h she was doing

2

a "I got the tickets."
b "Can/Could I see them?"
c "When are we leaving?"
d "You have (got) two days to get ready."
e "Do I need to bring any money?"
f "I'll pay for everything."
g "I'm going to buy some new clothes."

- h "Do you want to come/go with me?"
- i "I'll wait for you at home."

3

- a If I was/were the president of my country, I'd spend more money on the environment.
- b If I ever had the chance, I'd take a year off and go traveling.
- c If I could live anywhere in the world, I'd probably buy a beach villa in the Caribbean.
- d If I didn't need to learn English, I would have stopped a long time ago.
- e If I didn't have to go to work tomorrow, I would stay at home.
- f If I had been good at Math, I would have studied it at college.
- g If I had done more exercise when I was younger, I would be a lot healthier now.
- h If I'd been born with very rich parents, I wouldn't be doing this job.

4

- a If I'd studied harder at school, I'd have a better job.
- b If it was/were made of real gold, it would be worth a lot.
- c If they hadn't cornered the market, they wouldn't have put up the price.
- d If he didn't have a talent for seeing a gap in the market, he wouldn't have made millions.
- e If she had realized it was valuable, she wouldn't have given it away.
- f If my time wasn't/weren't so precious, I would have spoken to them.
- g If I hadn't been working late, I wouldn't have missed the movie.
- h If I had known you were coming, I would have come to meet you.

Vocabulary

1

a	office	d	action
b	a trash	e	a risk
c	a fortune	f	way

2

a	took	e	have / take
b	make	f	having
c	take	g	take
d	make; take	h	make

3

a	5	e	1	i	3
b	9	f	8	j	2
c	7	g	10		
d	6	h	4		

4

- a Expressions a/5, c/7, d/6
- b Expressions b/9, g/10
- c Expressions e/1, f/8, h/4, i/3, j/2

5

- a a steady stream of people
- b digest the information
- c use your time more profitably
- d food for thought
- e a half-baked idea
- f spare a couple of minutes
- g spent the evening
- h trickling slowly
- i wasting your time
- j worth your while

6

A

1	loaded	5	breadwinner
2	splash out	6	peanuts
3	blow	7	a rainy day
4	living	8	debt

B

1	worth	5	range
2	made	6	budget
3	pricey	7	stretch
4	hard		

7

- a I was looking for something a little more colorful.
- b I was wondering if you might have something a little less formal.
- c I was thinking of something a little more exciting.
- d I was hoping for something a little less expensive.
- e I'd like something that looks a little older.
- f I'd prefer something a little more fun.

Pronunciation

1

a	wealthy	d	special
b	whether	e	stretch
c	treasure	f	deluge

2

a	tʃ	c	ʒ	e	ʃ
b	dʒ	d	θ	f	ð

Writing

1

1. when
2. as soon as
3. While / As
4. then
5. after / as soon as
6. While
7. during
8. As soon as / When
9. until

2

totally - completely
Apparently - It seemed
Suddenly - Just then
frantically - desperately
finally - at last

4 Challenge

Grammar

1

- a had always wanted; saw
- b came; just closed; jumped
- c had been preparing; canceled
- d had never done
- e had been waiting; had finally arrived; didn't know
- f were getting; rang; told; had stolen

2

Aron Ralston had been climbing in a remote canyon in Arizona when disaster struck. He was climbing down a particularly narrow part when a huge rock fell and trapped his arm. As he had been climbing on his own, there was no one to help him. And he knew that no one would think of looking for him there because he hadn't told anyone where he was going. He <u>hadn't</u> brought his cell phone with him, so he couldn't call for help. He waited for five long days, but no one came to find him. By the fifth day, he <u>had</u> lost all sensation in his arm. He realized that he had no choice. He would have to cut his arm off at the elbow in order to save his life. Once he <u>had</u> cut off his arm, he managed to climb to the floor of the canyon. As he <u>was</u> walking out of the canyon, he met a group of people who <u>had</u> been hiking in the area. They called for help and a helicopter soon arrived to take him to a nearby hospital.

3

a What had Aron been doing when the accident happened?
b Why hadn't anyone come to look for him?
c Why hadn't he called for help?
d How long had he waited in the canyon?
e What had he done to get away?
f What had he been doing when he met the hikers?

4

a He had been climbing in a remote canyon.
b Because he hadn't told anyone where he was going.
c Because he hadn't brought his cell phone with him.
d He had waited in the canyon for five days.
e He had cut his arm off.
f He had been walking out of the canyon.

5

a have finished
b be going
c be working
d have had
e have gotten
f be going
g be playing
h have gotten; had

6

1 will/'ll be doing
2 will/'ll have started
3 will/'ll have made
4 will/'ll have fallen
5 will/'ll have given up
6 will/'ll be living
7 will/'ll have changed
8 will be running

Pronunciation

1

a up
b off
c down
d out
e off
f after

Vocabulary

1

a imminent
b shambolic
c interest
d deal
e genuine
f obscenely
g particularly

2

a self-conscious
b enjoyable
c reasonable
d self-discipline
e self-esteem
f accessible
g self-employed
h unbearable
i achievable
j doable

3

a self-conscious
b self-esteem
c enjoyable
d doable; achievable
e unbearable
f reasonable
g accessible
h self-discipline
i self-employed

4

a of
b jammed
c no
d out
e slow
f load
g into
h undo

5

1 figure out
2 undid the zipper
3 loaded the gun
4 in charge of
5 no way
6 swung into action
7 it / the gun jammed
8 go into slow motion

6

a feel
b picks
c give
d lit
e Look
f keep
g come
h taking

7

a coming down with
b put me off
c shake it off
d takes after him
e let you down
f get over it
g look into it
h do without it.

8

a It's horrible when that happens.
b It serves you right.
c You've only got yourself to blame.
d I'd go home if I were you.
e You look like death warmed over.

Listening

1

a To raise the media profile of the wildlife park.
b The confined space of the cage.
c No, she doesn't.
d Yes, she does.

2

a T
b F
c T
d F
e F
f F
g T
h T

3

a do some exercise
b give someone an idea
c go for a walk
d stay in shape
e raise money
f set a new record

5 Ritual

Grammar

1

1 find
2 decide
3 clear
4 *not possible*
5 *not possible*
6 do
7 spend
8 *not possible*

2

1 used to
2 didn't use to
3 didn't use to
4 used to
5 used to
6 used to
7 didn't use to
8 used to

3

1 *not possible*
2 wouldn't
3 wouldn't
4 would
5 would
6 would
7 wouldn't
8 *not possible*

4

1 used to be
2 would chase
3 found
4 tried
5 would hide
6 would always get
7 would have to
8 saw
9 had
10 'll/will always pay
11 'll/will play

5

a Could you remember to lock the door on your way out this morning, please?
b Do you remember telling me that I was the only person in your life?
c ✓
d It's so long ago that I've completely forgotten saying that. Did I really?
e ✓
f They stopped for a minute to get some money out at the bank on the way to the movies.
g This season, I'm going to try to win both the 100 and 200 meters.
h Try cooking it in oil – it'll taste a lot better.

Pronunciation

2

a two
b nerves
c irritating
d mind
e understand
f crazy

Vocabulary

1

1 jinxed
2 striding
3 outfit
4 derive
5 upper hand
6 renowned
7 rituals
8 immune
9 came across
10 crazy

2

a cozy
b urge
c slammed
d matches
e first
f domestic
g Force
h breakneck

3

a to do
b to get
c to go
d visiting / to visit
e to go
f being
g flying
h to get
i to do

4

1 complaining
2 insist
3 go
4 keeps
5 mad
6 telling

5

a I hate it when people tell me what to do.
b It really annoys me when people shout.
c The thing that annoys me most is a messy desk.
d I can't stand it when people keep me waiting.
e I find it irritating when nobody listens to me.
f Bad manners really get on my nerves.
g It's so annoying when it rains on the weekend.
h The way some people drive makes me crazy.

Writing

1

1 a
2 c
3 b
4 f
5 d
6 e
7 g
8 h

2

a Further to; in connection with
b caused directly by
c over the agreed price
d in due course
e furthermore
f unsuitable for this type of work

3

a legal advice
b a full refund
c the matter
d apology
e I will expect

4

Suggested answer

From most threatening to least threatening: a e b d c

6 Eat

Grammar

1

a ✓
b I've always hated
c I've been a vegetarian
d ✓
e I've done
f I've had
g ✓
h ✓

2

a have/'ve finished
b have/'ve been cooking
c have/'ve had
d has been eating
e have/'ve probably received
f have/'ve been talking

3

a She ~~has~~ got the job
b Callum hasn't been studying
c She hasn't ~~tell~~ told her parents yet.
d Alyson has been painting
e he has only ~~saw~~ seen
f Dan and Ursula have been getting ready

4

1 've been working
2 've been doing
3 started
4 got paid
5 've been promoted / was promoted
6 made
7 've accepted
8 've given
9 've moved

5

1 became
2 rose / had risen
3 was made
4 was discovered
5 was greeted
6 were made / had been made
7 was used
8 also ate
9 bought

6

a I am being helped with this exercise by a friend.
b My homework will be graded by my teacher.
c My dinner is being cooked by my sister this evening.
d I've never been given a ring.
e I will not / won't be forced to take an English examination.
f My dictionary hasn't been opened today.
g I was invited to a friend's house last weekend.

Pronunciation

1

/s/	/z/
ask beliefs extensive fussy loose restaurant this	always cheese dessert invisible noisy please these

Vocabulary

1

a 4
b 6
c 5
d 2
e 3
f 1

2

a raised
b shook
c stick
d held
e bending
f clenched

3

1 set
2 à la carte
3 vegetarian
4 regional
5 organic
6 dishes
7 paper
8 flavors

4

1 menu
2 dishes
3 light
4 fresh
5 extensive
6 flavor
7 three-course

5

1 The first and most obvious reason
2 In fact
3 As a result
4 What is more
5 Secondly
6 In other words
7 To sum up

6

1 so
2 Although / Even though
3 Furthermore
4 even though / although
5 Consequently
6 to sum up
7 However

7

a 1959
b 0.999
c 1/100th
d 23,302
e 1-800-446-5447
f 21st

8

a love
b oh
c oh
d zero
e zero

9

dark customers, chilled menu, overcooked customers

Listening

1

c Chestnut Wins Hamburger Olympics

2

a 24
b $20,000
c eight minutes
d 85
e 72
f peanut butter and toasted cheese
g hundreds
h 10,000

3

a wolfed down
b swallow
c get down
d stuff himself
e gorging on
f scarfing down

7 Escape

Grammar

1

a The travel agent suggested ~~us~~ that we go to the Florida Keys for our next vacation.
b He assured ~~to~~ us that we would have a wonderful time.
c He explained ~~us~~ that it had won an award for its clean beaches.
d He also mentioned ~~us~~ that it had a fantastic nightlife.
e He convinced ~~to~~ us that it was this year's top destination.
f Finally, he persuaded ~~to~~ us to book it by offering a discount.
g The company confirmed ~~us~~ that there would be no price increases.
h One week before departure, the company announced ~~us~~ that there was a 5% price increase.
i *correct*

2

a doing
b him to be
c me that
d that it
e that she was
f her to
g them to

3

a have to travel / need to travel
b could only
c had to book
d not/n't allowed to
e were allowed to use / could use
f couldn't park
g didn't have / need

4

1 the
2 -
3 a
4 the
5 the
6 the
7 a
8 the
9 a
10 the
11 the
12 the
13 -
14 The
15 a
16 a
17 the
18 a
19 the
20 -
21 The
22 a
23 -
24 the
25 -
26 the
27 the
28 a
29 the
30 the

5

a You can't measure ~~the~~ happiness.
b There never was ~~the~~ a good war or bad peace.

c Friendship is love with ~~the~~ intelligence.

d Men never remember, but ~~the~~ women never forget.

e ~~The~~ Money is power.

f Nothing is certain in ~~the~~ life except ~~the~~ death and taxes.

Vocabulary

1

a suggest
b advise
c assure
d reassure
e convince
f persuade
g mention
h claim

2

1 b
2 a
3 a
4 c
5 d
6 b
7 b
8 d

3

a ✓
b ✓
c ✓
d ✓
e -
f ✓
g -
h -
i ✓
j -

4

a endless
b careful
c helpful
d tasteless
e relentless
f doubtful
g childless
h stressful

5

a illegal
b illiterate
c impolite
d immature
e unwilling
f illogical
g undivided

6

1 should
2 well
3 views
4 recommend
5 won't
6 avoid
7 were
8 Whatever
9 must
10 sure
11 place

Writing

1

Topics mentioned: cost, entertainment, history, language, scenery (**a**, **b**, **e**, **g** and **j**)

2

a 3
b 5
c 4
d 1
e 2

8 Attraction

Grammar

1

a It is thought (that) they have had a fight.

b It is said (that) they are getting divorced.

c It is believed (that) an announcement will be made tomorrow.

d It has been suggested that Frances has taken the children to Los Angeles.

e It has been said (that) William wants custody of the children.

f It is believed (that) Frances has fallen in love with a younger man.

g It is thought (that) they will be getting married in the spring.

2

a Chocolate is thought to relieve stress.

b Blondes are believed to have more fun.

c Gray hair is thought to be attractive in men.

d Pale skin was said to be a sign of great beauty.

e Cosmetic surgery was once considered to be an expensive luxury.

f Brown eyes are believed to be stronger than blue eyes.

g Working in front of a computer screen is known to be bad for your eyes.

3

a I had my eyes tested last week.

b You need to get your bike fixed.

c You should get your hair cut.

d We're going to have this wall knocked down.

e The company is going to get its logo changed.

f We had the car checked last week.

4

a If you **were to find** some money on the street, what would you do with it?

b Would you have cosmetic surgery, **assuming** you had the money to pay for it?

c **Imagine** you could make a radical change to your lifestyle, what change would you make?

d Suppose **someone were to give** you three wishes, what would you wish for?

e **Supposing** you were to get the chance to spend an evening with the celebrity of your choice, **who would you choose**?

f What job would you like to do, **assuming** money, time, and talent were no object?

Pronunciation

2

a absent-minded
b big-headed
c easy-going
d good-looking
e level-headed
f open-minded
g self-centered
h laid-back

Vocabulary

1

a eye
b eyebrow
c cheekbone
d dimple
e jaw

2

a skin
b teeth
c eyes
d jaw
e smile
f nose
g cheekbones
h eyebrows
i lips

3

square jaw, turned-up nose

4

1 big
2 white
3 full
4 smooth
5 bone
6 high
7 dimples
8 eyebrows
9 eyes

5

a self-centered
b grown-up
c laid-back
d level-headed
e open-minded
f down-to-earth

6

1 self-centered
2 laid-back
3 level-headed
4 open-minded
5 down-to-earth
6 grown-up

7

a self-centered
b open-minded
c grown-up
d down-to-earth
e level-headed
f laid-back

8

a selfish
b tolerant
c mature
d unpretentious
e sensible
f relaxed

9

a caring
b stand-offish / unfriendly
c experienced / mature
d trustworthy / dependable
e mysterious
f straight

10

a did I put my foot in my mouth?
b get it off my chest
c made up his mind
d aren't from this neck of the woods
e a shoulder to cry on
f I'm up to my eyes (in work)
g play it by ear
h cost an arm and a leg

Listening

1

hobbies, family, tattoos, jewelry

2

a	F	c	F	e	F	g	T
b	F	d	T	f	F	h	T

3

a 1 I'm only kidding
2 I'm pulling your leg
b You're pulling my leg again, aren't you?
c I bet
d The same goes for
e Hold on
f Time's up

9 Genius

Grammar

1

a	must	d	could
b	couldn't	e	must
c	might	f	may

3

Some people think that the CIA may have ~~kill~~ killed President Kennedy. They say that Lee Harvey Oswald couldn't have been responsible for the shooting and the CIA may ~~be~~ have murdered him in prison as a way of stopping the investigation.

A survey in the US found that one in five people think that the Apollo astronauts ~~must~~ may never have landed on the moon. They think that the film of the event must have ~~being~~ been done with trick photography. Some people even believe that the government might have faked all the Apollo missions.

It has been suggested by some people that the US government could ~~has~~ have made secret contact with aliens. A mysterious crash at the Roswell military airport in 1947 may have ~~be~~ been an alien spacecraft. Since then, it is thought that the government may have kept another 11 similar incidents secret.

4

a -
b like
c -
d as if / as though
e as if / as though
f like
g -
h like

5

a ✓
b He appears to be asleep.
c It seems as if we've been here before.
d They look like rain clouds.
e The local people all seemed very friendly.
f ✓
g The bar looked cool, so we went in.
h You look as if you've seen a ghost.

Pronunciation

a	1 ii 2 i		d	1 i	2 ii
b	1 i 2 ii		e	1 i	2 ii
c	1 ii 2 i				

Vocabulary

1

a shiny
b run-down
c contemporary
d tough
e eccentric
f hideous
g derelict
h sprawling

2

a sprawling
b hideous
c derelict
d run-down
e contemporary
f eccentric

3

a	captivating	d	incentive
b	drizzling	e	enigmatic
c	endured	f	mere

4

1	When	6	During
2	soon	7	On
3	at	8	Just
4	From	9	after
5	Over	10	while

5

a	3	c	4	e	2
b	1	d	6	f	5

6

1 genetics
2 biology
3 scientist
4 science
5 economist
6 economic
7 mathematical
8 economics
9 physicist
10 mathematician
11 technological

7

- a He turned the dial on the thermostat to zero.
- b You can't turn it on until you've plugged it in.
- c How did people change channels before they invented remote controls?
- d Make sure the lid's on tight before you turn it on.
- e Put a cup under the place where the water comes out and push the blue button, OK?
- f Take the filter out of the holder and replace it after every cup of coffee that you make.

Writing

1

- a

2

California truck driver, Larry Walters, **has / had always wanted** to be a pilot.

... from a local store and **filled them / had them filled** with helium gas.

By now, he **was panicking**.

An airport helicopter eventually **succeeded** in bringing him back to earth.

3

- a plan
- b (epic) journey
- c purchased
- d seat
- e pistol

4

- a Larry Walters
- b be a pilot
- c join the US Air Force
- d weather balloons
- e weather balloons
- f garden chair
- g seat

5

Suggested answer

At the end of his act, the Argentinian magician, Professor Marvo, asked a male member of the audience who was sitting near the front to come on stage. The magician handed the man a gun and asked him to shoot him in the face. The man fired the gun and the magician then pulled the bullet from between his teeth.

The man was so impressed that he took another gun out of his pocket. While Professor Marvo was preparing to leave the stage, he said to him, "Catch this!" and shot him. He was killed instantly. Even during the subsequent trial, the man could still not understand why Professor Marvo (had) failed to catch the bullet.

10 Sell

Grammar

1

- a The most expensive advertisement of all time, which was for the drink Guinness™, cost $20 million.
- b It was made by Nicolai Fuglsig, whose other advertisements include the Sony Bravia advertisement.
- c ✓
- d ✓
- e Castlemaine XXXX, which is a kind of beer, once showed 17 different TV ads on one channel in one evening.
- f ✓
- g The longest advertising poster ever produced, which was made by O'Canada Gear© in Alberta, was over 332 m long.
- h ✓
- i Guy Ritchie, who used to be Madonna's husband, has directed a soccer ad for Nike™.
- j Nike™, which is one of the best known brands worldwide, spent more than $1.7 billion on advertising in one year.

2

- a that
- b who/that
- c who/that
- d that/which
- e that/which
- f whose
- g that/which
- h that/which
- i whose

In **d**, **e**, and **h** the relative pronoun can be omitted.

3

- a *Quantum of Solace*, which is the 22nd Bond movie, was first released in the UK.
- b Many Bond fans who enjoyed Daniel Craig's performance in *Casino Royale* are glad to see him back in the role of 007™.
- c Olga Kurylenko plays the role of a Russian-Bolivian agent who helps Bond in his search for revenge.
- d Mathieu Amalric plays the role of the villain who Bond has to try to stop.
- e The title of the movie is based on a short story which/that appeared in a collection called *For Your Eyes Only*.
- f The movie is directed by Marc Forster, who also directed the Oscar®-winning *Monster's Ball*.

4

Suggested answer

One day, Philip K. Wrigley, who was the founder of the famous chewing gum company, was sitting on a plane that was going to Chicago. During the flight, the man who was sitting next to him asked, "Why do you continue to advertise a chewing gum which is already the most popular in the world?" Wrigley, who was known for his wit, quickly replied, "For the same reason that the pilot of this plane, which is flying at 30,000 feet in the air, keeps the engine running."

5

- a What I wouldn't want is to be written about in the popular press.
- b It's only in the north of Canada that he's well known.
- c What I really hate is the way that celebrities always sound so sure of themselves.
- d The only thing that matters to some people is being on TV.
- e What I don't understand is why people take her so seriously.

Vocabulary

1

a	4	c	2	e	8	g	6
b	3	d	1	f	7	h	5

2

a I caught sight of his face for a split second as he walked past
b ✓
c I couldn't make out the details in the picture because the quality was so bad.
d ✓
e I gazed at the rain through the window for ages, thinking about what I'd say to her.
f ✓
g ✓
h Shh! They won't notice us if we just stand here and keep quiet.

3

a confidence
b tag
c cut
d conference
e image
f sector

4

a spending
b list
c revenue
d team
e name
f value

5

a stripped
b fussy
c care less
d fiercely
e epitomize
f rugged; heart-throb
g nostalgically
h haunting; conjuring up

6

1 cow
2 back
3 far
4 raking
5 placement
6 office
7 privilege
8 strike
9 clear
10 condition

7

a I get absolutely nervous before exams. ✗
b ✓
c His performance was very extraordinary. ✗
d That was definitely one of the best movies I've ever seen. It was totally good.✗
e ✓
f ✓
g The movie was pretty disappointing, but the party afterwards was extremely fantastic. ✗
h ✓
i That was some horror movie. I was very frightened to death. ✗
j Did you think so? I was extremely bored stiff. ✗

Pronunciation

2

a 2; 1
b 2; 1
c 1; 2

Listening

1

1 C
2 D
3 G
4 F
5 E
6 A
7 B

2

a 3, 5, 7
b 7
c 2, 4
d 3, 7

3

a 1 Could you call me on my cell phone?
2 Please call my assistant at 831- 749-2598.
3 Could you please call me back there?
4 Could you call me back?
b 1 I'll call again later.
2 I'll call back in half an hour.
c 1 I'm interested in
2 I'm calling about
3 I'm looking for

11 Student

Grammar

1

a will do
b going to fail; don't
c are coming
d has started; will be
e Will anyone try
f might
g are going to have; are
h 'm going to wait; know

2

a until the exams have finished
b I'll have finished
c I look
d finishes / has finished
e unless the weather changes
f I will probably have spent
g don't give

Pronunciation

1

a list
b feel
c book
d soon
e head
f learn
g course
h fan
i buzz
j heart

2

a /e/
b /ɑ/
c /i/
d /ʌ/
e /ɜr/
f /u/
g /æ/
h /ɔ/
i /ʊ/
j /ɪ/

Vocabulary

1

1 pay
2 heart
3 grades
4 higher
5 failed
6 course
7 applied
8 scholarship

2

a It is unlikely (that) he will study very hard.
b It is likely (that) he will fail most of his exams.
c He's bound to turn up without a pen.
d It's inevitable that he'll try and cheat.
e It's probable (that) he'll end up at the bottom of the class.
f He's not expected to go to college.
g It's unlikely (that) he'll get a good job.
h He's bound to get into trouble with the police.

3

a taste
b behind
c system
d senses
e make
f up to her

4

a mind-blowing; amazing
b mind; worried
c heaven; happy
d legs; exhausted
e burst; sad
f rope; desperate
g breath; amazed
h dying; thirsty
i door; sick
j stiff; afraid

Writing

1

1. a (F) n (I)
2. b (I) g (F)
3. c (I) f (F)
4. d (F) j (I)
5. e (F) m (I)
6. h (I) i (F)
7. k (F) l (I)

2

a Part 1: a, i
b Part 2: d, f, k
c Part 3: e
d Part 4: g

3

I was born ~~in a small town~~ not far from Mexico City, so my mother tongue is Spanish, but I have a good standard of spoken and written English, ~~because I have been going to an excellent language school near my town and I have been to the United States four times. I also had an Irish girlfriend for a couple of weeks~~.

I have an international driver's license ~~and I currently drive a red convertible Nissan™. I was going to work for a travel company here in Mexico last year~~, ~~but in the end~~ I worked for two months at the help desk at Mexico City Airport, where I had to deal with people from all over the world, ~~and sometimes I got to drive one of the airport buggies if there was a disabled passenger who needed some help. It was fun.~~

12 Home

Grammar

1

a overlooking
b walking
c taken
d watching
e cleaned
f read
g located

2

1. Sitting
2. going
3. occupying
4. admired
5. Fitted
6. specializing
7. known

3

1. many
2. several
3. few
4. no
5. plenty
6. little
7. hardly
8. most
9. enough
10. None
11. all

4

a of
b not
c ✓
d ✓
e of (second)
f ✓
g ✓
h the
i the (second)
j ✓

Vocabulary

1

a go next door
b fossil fuels
c central heating
d street cred
e fireworks display
f pitch dark

2

1. e
2. f
3. h
4. j
5. b
6. g
7. d
8. a
9. i
10. c

3

1. Well, I'd better be going. It was really good to see you.
2. Good to see you, too. Thanks for coming.
3. My pleasure. Thank you for inviting me.
4. Call me some time, OK?
5. I will. Give my regards to Betty, will you? Bye.

4

a latch
b shutters
c dustpan, brush
d parquet, tiles
e doormat
f blinds
g glazing
h sill
i bolt
j mantelpiece, ornaments
k hook
l outlet

Listening

1

a new homes / residential properties
b about 800
c four
d They have high walls and security cameras. They are guarded by dogs and armed security personnel.
e 26 million dollars

2

a T
b F
c F
d F
e T
f F

3

a crammed
b link-ups
c best
d not short of a buck or two
e armed

Notes

Notes

Notes

Notes

Notes

ISBN 9786685732504

9 786685 732504